Gabriella's Kitchen

Recipes & Tales from a Greek Island

Nimbus Publishing Limited
PO Box 9301, Station A
Halifax, NS   B3K 5N5
(902) 455-4286

Design: Graphic Detail Inc.

Dedication

To Bob Brooks, who was an exceptional person and a good friend.

Acknowledgements

Many thanks to my family and to my friend Thérèse Coughlan,
who helped me so kindly to deal with the hated computer.

Table of Contents

❧

Introduction

When I first saw the island of Corfu, in Greece, nearly forty years ago, it was simply paradise. Orange and lemon groves sloped right down to the beaches. Silvery olive trees and elegant cypresses, vineyards, and masses of wild flowers covered the whole island and fairly stunned you with their beauty. Smiling, hospitable people were always ready to greet you and ply you with grapes or figs or a glass of wine. In all the island, there were only one or two hotels and a couple of restaurants where the choice was grilled fish, grilled steak, salad, and boiled Swiss chard.

Full of enthusiasm and totally deprived of any experience, my husband and I rented a charming old Venetian villa. It was inaccessible and totally unsuited for a restaurant; so we promptly turned it into one. An ancient wall submerged in wisteria hid us very effectively from the road and possible clients, and the garden was so full of wild herbs and magnificent magnolia, pepper, olive and fruit trees that we had space for just a few tables. Not that it mattered! Tourists were a rarity in those days.

For a long time I cooked on a campfire and an old gas oven that would burst occasionally and singe my eyebrows. In the summer evenings, my kitchen would fill with so many fireflies that I always worried they would fall in my casseroles. In that old kitchen I was able to cook fresh tiger prawns the size of lobsters, free-range chickens, fruit and vegetables that never came near a pest killer or chemical fertilizer, absolutely fresh fish, and all sorts of things that disappeared long ago with the coming of "progress." Thanks to my husband's great way with people and his sense of humour, good cooking, and a pinch of luck, we gradually made a name for ourselves. We started having a good number of clients, many of whom became close friends and some of whom were quite famous.

One evening, for instance, at the very beginning, I was sitting in the restaurant with my husband waiting for guests. I happened to be reading a book by Sir Julian Huxley, and when we heard people coming I left it on the counter and fled to the kitchen. It was Sir Julian Huxley

◀ *To me, Corfu was simply paradise.*

Farmers still cut their hay by hand.

and his wife who came in, and the first thing he saw was his book on the counter! He was almost as tickled as we were. Gerald Durrell was also one of our regulars, and he and my husband Stephanos spent hours at a time exchanging jokes. A fair number of films were made in Corfu at the time, and we had stars like George Peppard, Paul McCartney, Albert Finney, Anouk Aymée, and many others. I was always rather shy with people, and my way of relaxing from work—which at times was staggering—was to sit in a corner of my kitchen with my knitting, embroidery, or patchwork. That's why I thought of combining cooking and patchwork, not with the intention of writing a comprehensive cookery book, but just to share some of my favourites with you: a real patchwork of recipes. You will find several starters, what the Greeks call mezédes, as they very often are the favourite Greek meal, and I tried to have as large a variety of them as possible. There are recipes for meat and fish, particularly those that were more popular with friends and clients; and a few desserts, since in Corfu we were blessed with such wonderful fresh fruit that we rarely bothered with anything else. If someone occasionally asked for a sweet dessert, I could concoct something simple and quick.

Speaking of simple, there is nowadays a tendency to make things as complicated as possible. You can go to a restaurant and have broiled duck slivers on a bed of caramelized radishes and mangoes, surrounded by a purée of Chinese water chestnuts with pesto sauce and topped with strawberry. Call it what you like, I call it a mess. If you keep things simple and always use absolutely fresh ingredients, you can't go wrong. I am sure your kitchen is perfectly equipped, so there are only two things I feel I can say from experience: first, keep everything clean and tidy while you cook, as cluttering it with dirty pans will only hinder your work and make you feel twice as tired.

Second, I am sure I could not have survived without a couple of large, heavy, cast-iron skillets. The larger the better, as these will accommodate your food easily, which is important especially with meat. Make sure the skillet is very hot before using it, so that the meat pores will seal very quickly and the juices remain inside, instead of flowing out into the pan (otherwise the meat will actually boil before having a chance to brown.) If you use very little fat, just enough to slightly coat the pan, you can grill meat quickly with excellent results, as cast iron stands very high temperatures much better than non-stick pans. They can also be used, of course, for fish and vegetables, for frying and deep-frying, for casseroles and sauces—in fact, for anything except boiling or steaming (for which you will need a different type of pot). I hope you will enjoy my recipes.

Gabriella Cristiani

Starters

In Greece, as in Turkey, starters are much more than the introduction to a meal; they very often are the meal, and, more than anything else, they are a Mediterranean way of life. The idea is to sit with your friends in the sun—or under the shade of a tree in summer—and have, in front of you, a little glass of ouzo accompanied by a large glass of icy water, or maybe retsina or white wine, and a selection of delicious little dishes. You alternate nibbling with lively discussions on politics, and every now and then stare lazily at the blue sea, or shout at the children (at the top of your voice) to keep them quiet. Very soon, the little dishes will be empty, and new ones will appear on the table with another bottle of wine or another bottle of ouzo. After repeating this operation two or three times, you rarely feel like a "proper" dinner, most international political problems are solved, and you head for home.

These little dishes are called mezédes; they may include olives, tiny fried fish, like fresh sardines or anchovies (delicious as they are and even better with a little skordaliá), boiled octopus (chopped in small bites with just a little olive oil and lemon or vinegar), fried inkfish, taramosaláta, tirópites (phyllo stuffed with goat cheese), a slice of spanakópita (phyllo pie with spinach, rice, and cheese, flavoured with dill), deep-fried zucchini or eggplants slices in batter, a slice of feta cheese, keftédes (small beef meatballs), meat and rice croquettes in tomato sauce, fried prawns, dolmádes (rice wrapped in vine leaves), satsíki (delicious creamy yogourt with chopped cucumber and dill or mint, very similar to the Indian raita), saganáki (a hard cheese rather similar to Romano, which is sliced, slightly floured, and fried), melitsanosaláta (basically the puréed pulp of roasted eggplant mixed with oregano, parsley, and finely chopped onion or garlic)—and even more if the restaurant is good and the cook is in the mood. As most of these mezédes are served with ouzo (a powerful drink flavoured with aniseed), a Greek restaurant without ouzo is almost like a café without coffee.

You can imagine my confusion when, one morning, some tourists appeared and ordered mezédes with ouzo. I was on my own at that moment and almost in tears with the shame of having to confess that we were out of ouzo. Just then my husband appeared, saw the situation in the bat of an eye, and went nonchalantly over to their table. As they chatted amiably, he asked what they had ordered and was told taramosaláta, fried zucchini, feta, and ouzo. He made a wry face and asked, "Taramosaláta with ouzo?" in such a way as to make it perfectly clear that the idea was inconceivable. He suggested white wine instead, and that was that. In Greek, they say, in these cases, something that translates into, "If he has a mind to, he can put horseshoes on fleas!"

◀ *Smiling, hospitable people were always ready to greet you.*

For cooking purposes, I find apple-mint is the best. I know you can find it in Canada because I have seen it sold in pots. It probably also grows wild, as it does in Europe. It has rounded, velvety leaves and a sweet flavour. Most other varieties, especially spearmint, have a more pungent and slightly pharmaceutical flavour that reminds me of toothpaste.

Spaghetti with Mint Sauce

½ kg spaghetti, spaghettini, or linguine
2 tablespoons olive oil
4 tablespoons butter
5 garlic cloves, crushed

1 teaspoon anchovy paste
½ cup chopped fresh apple-mint
1 cup freshly grated Parmesan cheese

Combine in a saucepan the olive oil, butter, anchovy paste, and garlic. After a minute or so, as soon as the garlic starts to colour, toss in the mint. Stir for a few moments. Take off the heat, and stir in the Parmesan. Pour this sauce over your spaghetti (cooked "al dente") and serve piping hot. You can add a little cream if you like. Serves 6.

St. Basil

"Basilikós" means "kingly," and basil, as its name suggests, reigns in all Mediterranean countries. You will find it in poetry and in sauces, in legends and in fairy tales, and on many sunny windowsills next to the beloved red geranium. In Greece, it takes on a saintly aura and is carried to church and to the cemetery on All Souls Day.

Being a good Italian, I used it lavishly in my cooking, and it grieved me that I was one of the very few people who could never grow it successfully in my garden. Many times our Greek customers complimented me and asked how did I make this or that sauce. When I mentioned basil, they looked at me in disbelief and seemed almost ready to spit it out. My husband was, at first, just as shocked as they were and explained to me its religious tradition. I went on using it and learned to keep quiet about it.

Basil is carried to church and to the cemetery on All Souls Day.

Pesto is a Genoese sauce made with lots of fresh basil and garlic. In Genoa, it is traditionally served with trenette, a homemade pasta, and is boiled together with a finely chopped potato. Because basil is difficult to find in the winter months, I gather it during the summer and preserve it in salt, covering it with plenty of olive oil to avoid contact with the air. This way, it keeps for months in the refrigerator. When I want to make fresh pesto, I simply add crushed garlic, grated Parmesan, butter or cream, and some crushed nuts to my preserved basil. Pine nuts are ideal, but walnuts, almonds, hazelnuts, and even groundnuts make interesting and cheaper substitutes. Pesto is excellent with pasta —especially spaghetti or linguine —but is also delicious with grilled fish or steak.

Pesto

2 cups fresh basil leaves
4-5 crushed cloves of garlic
$1/3$ cup pine nuts
1 cup grated Parmesan cheese

$1/3$ cup extra virgin olive oil
$1/2$ cup cream, or 2 heaping tablespoons butter

Combine the basil, garlic, butter, and nuts in a food processor. Pulse to form a coarse paste. With the machine running, gradually add the olive oil until the pesto reaches the desired consistency. This ready-for-use-pesto can be refrigerated for a few days. Makes about 2 cups.

La Marchesa

Whenever I think of pesto or basil, I remember the Marchesa. She was my very best and, at the same time, my most dreaded client. She had the finest palate, the nose of a hunting dog, and the curiosity of a cat. I never really cared to keep my recipes a secret, but with her I would have had the same chance as hiding a hippopotamus in a tea cup. She was a very charming and intelligent person, and often, if I was busy cooking, she came and chatted with me in the kitchen. I remember one evening I was frying fish in one pan and, in another,

Silvery olive trees and elegant cypresses dotted the countryside.

cooking meat with vinegar—the fumes and smells in the kitchen were so thick you could have cut them with a knife. Suddenly the Marchesa stopped talking and sniffed around. "What a divine smell of basil!" she said. "Aha, caught you this time," I thought. There was absolutely no trace of basil in the kitchen. Then she moved to the window, which opened directly onto the garden—and I remembered that just under the window I'd recently sown some basil, still so tiny it was barely visible. I am hanged if she did not spot it.

This paté can be prepared well in advance and will keep a long time if refrigerated—at least a week. It is very versatile and can be served with fresh or toasted bread, vols-au-vent, or crostini. It is ideal for snacks, for mixed hors d'oeuvres, or by itself. It also goes well on grilled steak or fillet. For a more formal presentation, it can be put in a mould and decorated.

Chicken Liver Paté

1 cup butter
1-2 tablespoons olive oil
1 cup coarsely chopped onion
1 $^1/_5$ cups chopped chicken livers
2 bay leaves

2 sage leaves, or $^1/_2$ tablespoon chopped thyme (fresh or dry)
$^1/_2$ cup sherry or white wine
1-2 tablespoons brandy
salt and black pepper to taste

Sauté the onions and herbs with half the butter and the olive oil over medium heat. When the onions become translucent, add the livers, salt, and pepper. As soon as they are brown and well cooked, stir in the sherry or wine, reduce the heat, and simmer for a few minutes. Discard the bay leaves and the sage. Add the remaining butter and let it melt, then add the brandy. Remove from the heat and purée in a blender or food processor until smooth and creamy. Taste for salt and pepper, and add a little more brandy if you like. Makes about 2$^1/_2$ cups.

Bruschetta (bruskétta) has become a fashionable starter. In its basic, original form, it is grilled or toasted fresh bread, rubbed with garlic and olive oil, and sprinkled with salt. This is so appetizing that restaurants in Rome often serve it free of charge to encourage your order! For a little variety, you can certainly add fresh tomatoes and herbs, or top with a variety of cheeses. My own favourite version remains the plain one.

Crostini are slices of toasted or grilled bread served with a variety of toppings: mozzarella and prosciutto, mozzarella with anchovies, pickled or braised baby artichokes, paté, bacon and cheese, mushrooms and bacon, mushrooms with sausage, etc. The following recipe comes from Tuscany and is one of the best versions.

Bruschetta and Crostini

3 chicken livers
3 tablespoons butter
3 tablespoons olive oil
2 finely chopped spring onions or chives
2 crushed cloves of garlic
1/2 teaspoon anchovy paste

A dash of white wine, or brandy, or vinegar
1 tablespoon capers
1 tablespoon fresh chopped parsley
8 slices of Italian bread cut 1/2-inch thick, then halved

Toss the livers in a skillet with the olive oil and butter, onions, garlic, and anchovy paste. Keep stirring, crushing the livers with a fork until well browned. Add a dash of white wine; you can vary this by using brandy or wine vinegar. Allow the liquid to evaporate (about a minute), then add the capers and chopped parsley. This mixture can be served as it is, or smoothed in a blender. Spread thinly on lightly toasted bread. Just before serving, put it under the hot oven grill for a couple of minutes. Serves 4.

❧ *Keep an eye out for zucchini flowers at your local market. You want the sterile male flower that looks rather like a lily and has a fairly long stalk. Shake the flower gently to remove any dirt or insects, and trim the stems to about two inches. To stuff them, I use the triangular, creamy cheeses of "La vache qui rit" type, chopped finely, which works very well. You could also use fontina, fresh Italian mozarella, or bocconcini.*

Stuffed Zucchini Flowers

12-16 large zucchini flowers
vegetable oil for deep frying
Filling:
1 1/2 cups cheese, finely cut
1 beaten egg
1 heaping tablespoon fresh chopped
  apple-mint

Batter:
1 cup flour
1 egg
a pinch of salt
enough beer to obtain a thick consistency

Let the batter rest for an hour or so before using. Combine the cheese, egg, and mint in a small bowl. Gently open the petals of each flower and spoon in the filling, about one full teaspoon for each flower. Heat the oil in a small cast iron pan as it is better to fry them a few at a time. Holding the flowers by their stem, dip them in the batter one at a time and deep-fry for a few minutes, turning once, until crisp and golden-brown. Sprinkle with salt. Drain on paper towels and serve at once.

A Cock-Eyed Idea!

The first time I prepared stuffed zucchini flowers, I certainly had no intention of making them a regular dish. As often as possible I tried new things to keep clients interested, and almost every time I had fights with my husband about it. Like most Greeks, he was very traditional about food. I never expected that people would fall in love with my flowers and keep asking for more. How many times I regretted my idea, I can't tell you! We had to go through zucchini fields before sunrise to collect them. As the day grows warmer, their petals shut firmly tight and all the King's horses won't make them change their mind. When you have to stuff hundreds of them, you want to catch them at the right time. Zucchini leaves are very rough and scratch your skin, and my husband kept grumbling and cursing my cock-eyed ideas. By the time we left the zucchini fields, we were both in a black mood. There was no going back, though, or people would grumble!

We went to the zucchini fields before sunrise.

This was George Peppard's favourite dish. The first evening he came, he had it for dinner, and he came to the kitchen and kissed me. After that, he came back every evening while he was in Corfu and always had the same prawns.

Unless I have really good, sun-ripened, fresh tomatoes, I use tomato juice for sauces. It is tasty and saves me from having to crush or process whole tinned tomatoes. Remember you should never cook tomatoes (or other acidic ingredients like lemon or vinegar) in aluminium pans.

Prawns alla Marinara

Rice ring

To serve prawns in a rice ring, cook the rice a little in advance, mix it with a bit of butter to prevent it from sticking, and press it firmly in a well-buttered ring-shaped mould. Cover with tinfoil and keep warm in a low oven. Just before serving, un-mould the rice onto a large serving dish and put your prawns, with their sauce, in and around the rice ring, decorating with parsley, sliced tomatoes, or peppers.

5-6 tablespoons olive oil
24 large prawns, shelled and deveined
5-6 crushed garlic cloves
1-2 fresh chili peppers
2 tablespoons dry oregano or thyme
2 cups tomato juice
2 heaping tablespoons freshly chopped parsley and salt to taste

Heat half the olive oil in a large heavy skillet over high heat. For this, as for most other uses, I always prefer a cast iron pan. When the oil is hot, toss in the shelled de-veined prawns with their tails on. Make sure they are not over-crowded in the pan or they will end up steamed rather than seared. If necessary, sauté them in batches. Remove the prawns as soon as they turn pink and set aside. Sauté the garlic and chili with the remaining oil, until the garlic begins to brown, and then stir in the tomato juice, salt, and oregano. Bring to a boil, then simmer until the juice is slightly thickened. Add the prawns, sprinkle with parsley, and cook just long enough to heat through. Serves 6.

Tuna Mockfish and Mayonnaise

*1 tin of tuna fish, about 170 grams,
    preferably canned in olive oil*
2 cups of mashed potatoes
1 tablespoon anchovy paste
1 crushed clove of garlic
1 tablespoon Dijon mustard

*1 heaping tablespoon of fresh chopped
    parsley*
1 tablespoon finely chopped chives
3-4 tablespoons wine vinegar
2 heaping tablespoons capers
salt and pepper to taste

Mix all the ingredients thoroughly with a fork. Shape this mixture into a fish shape onto a serving dish, using a wet spoon. Try to fashion fins and a swishing tail, or you can use a fish-shaped mould, slightly oiled. Just before serving, cover the fish with homemade mayonnaise and decorate with lettuce, lemon slices, strips of red and yellow peppers, etc. Don't forget two capers for the eyes! Serves 6.

Recipe for mayonnaise appears on page 36.

An old saying advises to use mussels and other shellfish only in the months that contain an "R"; that is, from September to April. I think this applies only to people like Italians, who eat mussels raw like oysters. Still, why not stay on the safe side and follow this advice?

Mussel Soup

6 tablespoons olive oil
5 lb mussels in the shell, scrubbed and
   carefully cleaned of their "beard"
$^1/_3$ cup finely chopped shallots or
   spring onions
6 crushed garlic cloves
1 fresh chili pepper, whole — if you like it
   really hot, chop it finely

1 tablespoon chopped fresh oregano (or
   1 teaspoon dried oregano)
3 cups tomato sauce
$^1/_3$ cup chopped fresh parsley
$^1/_2$ cup white wine, dry
salt to taste

Garlic Croutons

To make garlic croutons, toast lightly 1-inch thick slices of good fresh bread. Rub both sides with garlic and olive oil, and cut the bread into cubes. Just before serving, toss the cubes quickly in a heavy skillet, or put under a hot grill until golden and fragrant.

Lightly coat a large skillet or casserole with oil. Add the mussels and cook on high heat for a few minutes, shaking the pan occasionally, until most of them open. Remove from the heat, discard any mussels that failed to open, and shell the rest. If you like, save a few shells for decoration. Save the juice left in the pan and strain through a fine sieve to remove any grit. Wipe the skillet clean and add the remaining oil. Over medium heat, sauté the shallots, oregano, chili and garlic. As the garlic starts colouring, add the wine and the mussel juice, and cook a few minutes more to allow the wine to evaporate. Add the tomato juice, and salt to taste. Bring to a boil, reduce heat, and simmer a few more minutes. Stir in the mussels and the parsley. When well heated through, serve immediately, garnished with a few shells, croutons, and fresh parsley. Serves 4-6.

You often have to discard almost half the artichoke leaves, unless they are very tender specimens. You can set them aside and use them for soup, throwing out only the furry part.

Artichokes and Potatoes Corfu Style

6 artichokes
2-3 tablespoons lemon juice
6 tablespoons olive oil
1 large onion, chopped finely
1 garlic clove, crushed
6 small potatoes or 4 medium ones, peeled
  and quartered

1 cup hot water
2 tablespoons fresh chopped dill
1 tablespoon chopped fresh apple-mint
2 tablespoons fresh chopped parsley
salt and pepper to taste

Clean the artichokes, eliminating all the tough leaves and furry centres. Quarter and soak them in a bowl of cold water with the lemon juice to prevent discolouration; do the same with the potatoes. Heat the oil in a large heavy-bottomed casserole. Add the garlic, onion, dill, and mint and sauté for a couple of minutes. Stir in the drained artichokes and potatoes, and cook on medium heat until nicely browned all over, stirring frequently. Add the water, salt, and pepper, and simmer until the vegetables are tender and the liquid reduced to a thick sauce. A little more water may be necessary, added a few drops at a time. Sprinkle with the parsley, and serve hot. Serves 6-8.

Taramá, the base of this dish, is specially-prepared cod's roe and should be bright reddish-pink. You will find it in a good Greek delicatessen. Serve this creamy, pungent spread on toast or fresh Italian bread, or offer it as a dip with raw vegetables.

Taramosaláta

1 cup bread, soaked first in cold water,
*   then squeezed dry*
1 teaspoon taramá

2-3 crushed garlic cloves
2-3 tablespoons fresh lemon juice
olive oil, about 1/2 cup or to taste

Put the bread, taramá, and garlic in a blender. Pulse to combine and gradually add a little lemon juice and oil alternately, until it reaches the consistency of a thick cream. Store, covered, in a refrigerator until ready to use.

This can hardly be called a recipe, but it is a good suggestion!

Arugula with Mayonnaise

The arugula available in Canada has a much milder flavour than that of Greece. I would add a little garlic to the mayonnaise, or rub the salad bowl with a garlic clove.

Fresh arugula and mayonnaise is a delicious combination. Sliced fresh button mushrooms or a few slivers of Parmesan cheese can be added for tasty variations. Served with tiny croutons, this makes a good starter. For mayonnaise, see page 36.

These can be served with a variety of hors d'oeuvres, or accompany grilled or boiled meat.

Roasted Peppers

Choose large, firm, green, red and yellow bell peppers. Clean them, remove the seeds, and cut in one-inch wide strips. Toss them with a little olive oil and salt, and roast or grill in a medium-hot oven until brown and fork-tender. Remove the charred outer skin and place in a serving dish with a few drops of olive oil, some capers, crushed garlic, and salt and pepper to taste. A few black olives make this simple appetizer even more colourful.

 A good starter, especially if followed by a light main course.

Finocchi au Gratin

6 medium fennel bulbs
1 cup flour
3 cups milk
3 tablespoons butter

$^1/_2$ teaspoon salt
$^3/_4$ cup Parmesan cheese, grated
2-3 teaspoons breadcrumbs
black pepper or dry chili pepper to taste

Clean and halve the fennel, removing the tough outer skin and feathery leaves—all except the most tender. Blanch for five minutes in boiling water, and drain. Meanwhile, prepare a white sauce by whisking well the flour in the cold milk. Add salt and butter and cook on medium heat, stirring constantly with a wooden spoon until the sauce thickens. Remove from the heat and stir in the Parmesan. Place the finocchi in a buttered oven dish and cover with the white sauce. Sprinkle with breadcrumbs and pepper, and bake in a pre-heated oven at 375°F until golden brown, about 30 minutes. Serves 4-6.

A dish apparently well appreciated by this Turkish gentleman who lived in Greece during the Ottoman occupation. An "imam" is a religious leader.

Eggplants Imam Baldi

6 medium-sized eggplants
6 garlic cloves, chopped finely
6 teaspoons capers
$^{1}/_{2}$ cup freshly grated romano or
   Parmesan cheese
$^{1}/_{2}$ cup fresh breadcrumbs

2 tablespoons chopped fresh parsley
1 tablespoon oregano
$^{1}/_{2}$ cup olive oil
2-3 cups tomato juice
salt and freshly ground black pepper

Trim the stalk ends of the eggplants. Use a sharp paring knife to peel the skins, leaving a few thin strips of skin intact on the side of each eggplant, which will prevent the vegetables from collapsing during cooking. Cut 4 or 5 deep slits in each eggplant. In a mixing bowl, combine the garlic, capers, cheese, breadcrumbs, and herbs. Season with salt and pepper, and divide the mixture between the eggplants, pressing it deep into the incisions. Heat the olive oil in a large, heavy-based skillet over medium heat, and brown the eggplants all over. Add the tomato juice and bring to a simmer. Cook for 20-30 minutes with the lid on, until the eggplants are tender and the sauce thickened. Season to taste, and serve hot. Serves 6.

The Arabian Prince

One summer evening, I saw an apparition. There wasn't much work, and I was sitting in the garden with some friendly clients, enjoying the perfume of orange blossom and jasmine, when an apparition rose in front of our eyes. A young couple walked in —easily the most beautiful people I'd ever seen — followed, a few paces back, by an elderly lady. They were an Arabian prince, his wife, and the wife's chaperone, who never left her for a minute. He was dressed in a white silk tunic and a turban, and she was wrapped in gauzy white veils with bracelets on her wrists and ankles, so that she tinkled as she moved. There was a sparkle of diamonds both in their eyes and on their clothes. We all just stood and gaped. I have forgotten their names, but I will never forget them. After their dinner, the Princess bought some of my appliqué pictures, for which the Prince gave us a princely sum.

After dinner, the Princess bought some of my appliqué pictures.

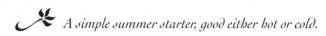 *A simple summer starter, good either hot or cold.*

Stuffed Tomatoes

6 large ripe tomatoes
6 tablespoons arborio rice
6 tablespoons chopped fresh basil

· olive oil, salt and pepper to taste
· 1 cup tomato juice or water
·

Pre-heat the oven to 375°F, and lightly grease a baking dish. Remove the tops from the tomatoes, slicing about a third off. Spoon out the flesh and seeds, chop coarsely, and place this in a bowl with the rice, basil, salt and pepper, and a drizzle of olive oil. Fill the tomatoes with this mixture and replace the "lids." Sprinkle with more olive oil and about one cup of water or tomato juice. Bake for about 30 minutes, checking the liquid from time to time; add more if needed so they do not become too dry before the rice is cooked. You can replace the basil with oregano or thyme. Serves 6.

 These make quick, easy starters or party snacks, and can be prepared several days in advance.

Quick Tirópites

Roll puffed pastry (ready-made is excellent) to ⅛-inch thickness and cut into round or square shapes. Cook in a pre-heated oven, at 400°F for 20 to 25 minutes until golden and puffy. Cool on a rack. (Fresh croissants provide a quick and easy substitute.) Cut the pastries horizontally in half, and spread each half with creamy cheese. Store back to front, wrapped in saran wrap, and keep refrigerated until needed. At the last moment, spread a small amount of anchovy paste over the cheese, just a dot, and cook under a hot oven grill for a few minutes until golden brown. A little paté, prosciutto, or bacon works equally well. Serve immediately.

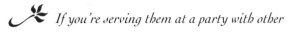 *If you're serving them at a party with other*

mixed hors d'oeuvres, you can use smaller mushrooms.

Stuffed Mushrooms

6 large mushrooms (Portobello or any
large mushrooms)
6 tablespoons olive oil
1 teaspoon butter
3-4 crushed garlic cloves
2 bacon rashers, chopped

2 spring onions, finely chopped
¹/₂ cup fresh breadcrumbs
¹/₂ cup grated Parmesan cheese
1 tablespoon brandy
1 tablespoon chopped fresh parsley
salt and pepper to taste

Gently detach the stalks from the caps. Chop the stalks finely and sauté them in a hot, heavy skillet with the oil, butter, garlic, bacon, and onions, for a few minutes. Remove from the heat and add the parsley, Parmesan, breadcrumbs, and brandy, and season with salt and pepper. Stir well together and fill the mushroom caps with this mixture, pressing it well. Place in a well-buttered oven dish and sprinkle with a few more drops of olive oil or melted butter. Bake in a moderate oven or under a grill until well browned. Serves 6.

These sweet and sour onions are perfect in mixed hors d'oeuvres or as an accompaniment to grilled or boiled meat. They can be prepared well in advance, and are tasty either hot or cold.

Sweet and Sour Baby Onions

2 cups baby red onions
2 tablespoons butter
2 tablespoons olive oil

1 heaping tablespoon sugar
$1/5$ cup wine vinegar
salt and freshly ground black pepper

Blanch the onions in boiling water for 1 minute, then drain and cool; this makes peeling easier. Sauté with the butter and olive oil in a large, heavy-based skillet for a few minutes, shaking the pan occasionally. When the onions are browned and tender, increase the heat and sprinkle with sugar, salt, and pepper. Stir until they begin to caramelize, add the vinegar, and simmer for a few minutes more until the vinegar evaporates.

Three Variations on Chicken Soup

❦

Augholémono

This delicious soup from Greece is both nutritious and easily digested, perfect if you are feeling under the weather.

6 cups homemade chicken stock
³/₄ cup arborio rice
4 eggs
4-6 tablespoons lemon juice
salt to taste
grated Parmesan cheese to serve

Cook the rice in the boiling stock for 15 minutes. Turn the heat off and let the soup rest 5 more minutes or until the rice is really soft and tender. Beat the eggs with the lemon juice in a bowl, and add about half a cup of the boiling broth, a little at a time, until the mixture is well dissolved. Pour back into the soup and serve immediately with abundant Parmesan cheese. Serves 4-6.

Stracciatella (stratchate'lla)

This is the simplest and quickest of all soups and is delicious. Traditionally you use one egg per person, but if you want to reduce this amount for dietary reasons, three eggs could do for six people, with no change to the other ingredients.

6 cups good homemade chicken stock
3 to 6 eggs
6 heaping tablespoons fresh breadcrumbs and/or semolina
1 teaspoon grated lemon zest, or ¹/₂ teaspoon grated nutmeg
salt and pepper to taste
6 heaping tablespoons grated Parmesan cheese

Bring the stock to a boil. Meanwhile, beat together the eggs, Parmesan, breadcrumbs and/or semolina. Add to the boiling stock and stir for one minute. Remove from the heat and let it sit a few minutes. Season with lemon zest or nutmeg and taste for salt and pepper. Serves 6.

Zuppa Pavese

This soup comes from Pavia, a city in Lombardy in the North of Italy. It was very popular at the turn of the century, in my grandmother's time; it then disappeared from the scene.

Place a slice of toast in each individual soup bowl. Sprinkle it with grated nutmeg or lemon zest and 2 tablespoons of grated Parmesan cheese. Break a really fresh egg onto the toast and pour boiling broth over it. The egg will be cooked but deliciously soft, like a poached egg. It is important that the broth be really on the boil.

I like to decorate each individual soup bowl with a small mound of mashed potatoes in the centre (which can be shaped with a cookie mold or a small cup), and to adorn it with a sprig of herbs, or a carrot slice, or a teaspoonful of peas, etc.

Soup Nausicaa

2 large onions, coarsely chopped
6 medium zucchini, coarsely chopped
4 medium potatoes, peeled and chopped
milk as needed, about 2-3 cups

2 tablespoons butter, or $1/2$ cup cream
$1/2$ cup chopped fresh parsley
salt and pepper to taste

Place the vegetables in a casserole with just enough water to cover them. As soon as they are tender, add an amount of milk roughly equal to that of the water, salt, and pepper. Blend in a food processor, return to the stove, and bring to a boil, stirring constantly with a wooden spoon as the mixture tends to stick to the bottom of the pan. Just before serving add the butter (or cream) and the parsley. Serves 6-8.

You can replace the zucchini with asparagus, peas, lettuce (just the harder outside leaves, reserving the tender hearts for salads), celery, spinach, or artichokes (the leaves you discard when you prepare them for other purposes), and you will have equally tasty soups.

There are many versions of this soup throughout the world, from India to North Africa to Italy and France, and so on. This recipe comes from Tuscany.

Lentil Soup

1 ¹/₂ cups lentils
1 large onion, finely chopped
2 crushed cloves of garlic
5 or 6 tablespoons olive oil
1 teaspoon fresh or dry chopped thyme

1 heaping teaspoon dry rosemary, very
    finely chopped
2 cups tomato juice
stock to taste
salt to taste

Soak the lentils in cold water for a couple of hours, then rinse thoroughly. Place the onion, garlic, herbs, and olive oil in a heavy-bottomed pan. Cook on moderate fire, stirring occasionally with a wooden spoon. Add the drained lentils, and toss them together until they are evenly coated with oil. Top with hot water, enough to cover the lentils with ¹/₂ an inch to spare. Cover with a lid and simmer on low heat until the lentils are very tender; if necessary, add more hot water, a little at a time. At this stage add the tomato juice, salt and pepper to taste, and one cup of hot stock or water. Bring quickly to a boil and turn off the heat. Let the soup rest a few minutes before serving. This soup is rather thick; you can add as much stock as you like to reach the density you want. Serves 6-8.

Bread

❧

I learned how to make bread in Italy during the war, when I was about eleven. We were evacuated to a small country village where it was easier to survive; in town, people starved. I often watched the peasants making wonderful homemade bread, and was delighted when I learned to make it myself. I still make it whenever I can, as it is really quite easy, and so different from the bread that you buy! When it is fresh and straight out of the oven, it is one of the best things you can eat.

In a large china or enamel basin, measure about 9 ¹/₂ cups of flour with 1 tablespoonful of sea salt, preferably not too fine. Set this aside while you dissolve 2 heaping tablespoons of granulated yeast in 4 cups of warm or lukewarm water and sprinkle with a tiny pinch of sugar. Wait until the yeast starts foaming—I like to wait at least half an hour—and then stir into the flour. With a spoon or directly with your hands start working the dough, adding more tepid water if needed, until you have a soft dough. Place the dough onto a floured board and keep working it, pushing it well with the palm of your hands, giving it half a turn, and pushing again. Work and turn the dough all round, until it becomes homogeneous and elastic, at least ten or fifteen minutes. To avoid it sticking to your hands, rub them often with a little flour, and sprinkle dough and table with a little more; remember, though, that the softer the dough, the lighter your bread will be. Shape into a ball and, with the tip of a sharp knife, trace a cross on the top. Put in a well-floured or lightly greased container, and let the dough rest and rise in a warm place protected from drafts, for at least 2 hours or more, until it has doubled in size. A little overtime won't do the dough any harm, but a little less may easily spoil your bread.

Put the dough on a floured board and flatten by hitting it with the palm of your hand a few times. Work it again a few minutes, divide into four parts, and shape each part into an oblong shape. Again with the tip of a sharp knife, cut a few slits diagonally on the surface, and place on lightly-greased oven trays. Cover the dough with a clean tea cloth and let it rest again for at least one or one-and-a-half hours. In the meantime, pre-heat the oven to maximum. Put your bread in and turn the oven down to 450°F. Cook without opening the oven for 25-30 minutes, after which it should be ready. Insert a knife in the bread, and check that the blade comes out clean. Remove the bread, resting it on a rack until it cools down. Once cold, you can wrap it in cling-wrap and freeze it, so you won't have to do your baking too often.

Pizza

ou can make pizza with the same dough, without any extra ingredients except for the topping. After the first rising, use a rolling pin to roll down the dough to about a half-inch thick, or a little less if you like your pizza crisp and crusty. The simplest topping is tomato juice, thin cheese slices (fresh Italian mozzarella is by far the best), a sprinkle of dried or fresh oregano, a few fresh basil leaves, and a drizzle of virgin olive oil. I also add freshly crushed black pepper and a little salt, but it's up to your taste. You can use any number of toppings on pizza: black olives, anchovies, lightly braised bell peppers, mushrooms, prosciutto, bacon, herbs, different cheeses, and of course garlic. Don't smother it in cheese, and please don't use the type of salami called "pepperoni"; instead, substitute it with thin slices of fresh Italian sausage.

Another perfect day for picking flowers.

Fish

In my youth, the Mediterranean was uncontaminated and full of fish. In certain places the water was so crystal clear you felt like drinking it; actually, you did drink it. I remember as a young girl I saw a fisherman in Capri having a snack in his boat. He cut a slice of bread, dipped it in the sea, rubbed it with half a tomato and ate it. It seemed a very good idea. I myself cooked spaghetti on the beach in Corfu using sea water, and it was perfect. Imagine doing a thing like that now! I was glad to see that in Nova Scotia there are still plentiful fish, including lovely lobsters.

Speaking of lobsters, you can believe me when I say that you don't have to boil them alive. You can freeze them for 2-3 hours, chop their head off, drop them in boiling water, and no one will know the difference.

Many people think they don't like anchovies, but they do, they simply love them —provided they do not see them. In our restaurant it happened hundreds of times, with hundreds of people, so I can assure you it is true. Try it yourself — and don't tell your guests. The ancient Romans lavishly used anchovy sauce as a base for practically every dish they ate. Nowadays you find anchovies in all Mediterranean cooking, from Salade Niçoise to pizzas, crostini, Vitel tonnè, etc.

Rolled Sole Fillets

6 medium-sized fillets of sole
6 garlic cloves, crushed
4 tablespoons capers
6 tablespoons grated Parmesan
6 tablespoons fresh chopped parsley

6 teaspoons breadcrumbs
1 teaspoon anchovy paste
4 tablespoons olive oil or melted butter
salt and pepper to taste

Combine all the ingredients together, except the fish and the oil or butter. Mix well, and spread some paste on each fish. Roll the fillets up, securing them with one or two toothpicks. Arrange these rolls in a greased baking dish, drizzle with the olive oil or butter, and bake or grill in the oven for about 15 minutes until the fish is well browned. Serves 6.

You can use any white fish fillets for this dish, but my favourites are sole or bass.

Fillets of Sole or Bass with Mint and Almonds

6 large sole or bass fillets, floured
1 cup almonds, crushed finely
(to the size of sesame seeds)
1-2 eggs
3 tablespoons butter

6 tablespoons olive oil
$^{1}/_{2}$ cup whipped cream
6 teaspoons fresh chopped apple-mint
1 teaspoon lemon zest
salt and freshly ground black pepper

Have the flour and crushed almonds ready on separate plates; stir in a tablespoon of flour with the crushed almonds. Beat the egg—start with one, and if it's not enough add another. Roll each fillet first in the flour, then in the beaten egg, and finally in the crushed almonds, pressing the fillets well into the mixture to coat on both sides. Heat the olive oil and butter in a large cast iron pan, and fry the fillets two or three at a time on medium heat, until nicely browned on both sides. Place the fish on a warm serving dish. Meanwhile, whip the cream stiff, stir in the mint and the lemon zest, and put a dollop of it on each fish. Serves 6.

Of Men & Fish

❧ There is always a strong attachment between the sea and the men born near it, but the love for fish you find in Greece is rather unique. On their way to the office or driving to a party, Greek gentlemen will stop dead in their tracks if they see a fishing boat land with its catch. They will examine and discuss at length every type of fish, and leave reluctantly. The wives do all the shopping and household chores, but when it comes to shopping for fish, it's the man of the house who goes to the market. I heard big burly men talk about fish with the tenderness of a mother.

In summer, everybody naturally liked to eat in the garden.

Whereas a Northern European is often repulsed by the sight of fish served whole with head and all, a Greek or an Italian will look suspiciously at a mere fillet, and ask if it's frozen.

Real connoisseurs maintain that the cheek is the best part of fish. I often watched indulgently as they went for it, even if it was a small sardine. Well, they are quite right! We were once given a splendid bass as a present, a huge specimen weighing 14 kilos. With its cheeks we made a meal for several people, and it was indeed the most delicious thing.

The name of this dish comes from the word ail,

French for "garlic." With Bouillabaisse and Bourride, this

is a great classical dish of Provence.

Aioli

This sauce is essentially fresh mayonnaise (see recipe on page 36) made with lemon juice, with the addition of raw crushed garlic. For a very refined version you can add the raw red flesh of sea urchins, crushed, or a few spoonfuls of boiled crab or lobster. In the South of France (as in Greece with skordaliá) it constitutes a whole sumptuous meal as it is served with boiled, grilled, or fried fish (traditionally it must include salt cod) and a variety of salads and boiled vegetables like beans, or Swiss chard. Boiled potatoes and red beetroot are always present. Of course, you can use it with any fish you like, with the exception, in my mind, of trout or salmon, whose delicate flavor is better accompanied by butter or cream-based sauces rather than garlic and olive oil. You don't have to make a really fierce aioli, but don't stint on the garlic, either. I suggest about two cloves of crushed garlic for one cup of mayonnaise.

This citrus butter is also very good with boiled lobster.

Grilled Salmon Steaks
with Orange and Lemon Butter

6 medium-sized salmon steaks
6 tablespoons olive oil
$^1/_2$ cup butter
$^1/_4$ cup fresh lemon juice
4 tablespoons fresh orange juice
1 tablespoon Cointreau

1 teaspoon each grated lemon and
   orange zest
salt and freshly ground black pepper
4 sprigs of fresh mint
lemon and/or orange wedges to serve

Preheat the oven grill to 375°F. Brush the salmon on both sides with olive oil and grill or pan-fry until the fish is brown and cooked through, about 10-15 minutes, depending on the thickness of the fish. Meanwhile, in a mixing bowl, whisk together the cold butter, lemon and orange juices, Cointreau, and citrus zest. Season to taste with salt and pepper. Cover the grilled steaks with the mixture, and garnish with the mint sprigs and citrus wedges. Serves 6.

Skordaliá consists simply of mashed potatoes, salt, a little olive oil, and lemon juice, and as much raw crushed garlic as you can take. In Greece it is made often with pestle and mortar, and the potatoes become rather gluey. I prefer to prepare ordinary, fluffy, mashed potatoes and then add the other ingredients. In Greek restaurants or homes, this is traditionally served with fish (grilled, fried, or boiled) and accompanied by salads or boiled vegetables such as French beans or Swiss chard. Personally I like it also with grilled or roasted meat, especially lamb. You can also serve it as a dip with croutons or raw vegetables.

Skordaliá (from the Greek skórdos, or garlic)

2 cups mashed potatoes
6 tablespoons virgin olive oil

3-6 cloves of crushed garlic, to taste
salt and lemon juice to taste

Combine all the ingredients together, adding oil, lemon, and garlic a little at a time and tasting often until you find the result satisfactory. Makes about 2 cups.

Accompanied by a little skordaliá or aioli it's even better. If you prefer, you can fry the croquettes in the same batter as for Stuffed Zucchini Flowers (page 8).

Salt Cod or Stockfish Croquettes

¹/₂ cup olive oil for frying
2 cups fish, soaked and flaked
2 cups mashed potatoes
2-3 eggs
flour to coat

breadcrumbs to coat
1 heaping tablespoon chopped fresh
  parsley
2 tablespoons lemon juice

Soak the fish in abundant cold water overnight. The next morning, drain and cover with fresh cold water again, and leave for another hour or two. At this stage it will be soft enough to be cleaned easily. Get rid of the skin and bones carefully checking that no bones are left. If you find fillets already cleaned, even better. Flake the fish with a fork. Mix in a large bowl with the mashed potatoes, one egg, and the parsley. Shape into round balls, each about the size of a large walnut. Beat the remaining two eggs in a soup dish with the lemon juice. Coat each fish ball first in flour, then in the beaten egg, then in breadcrumbs. Flatten them slightly with the palm of your hand. Heat the oil in a heavy 8-inch skillet (I use a small one for frying fish, to save on the oil) and fry the fish, on moderate heat, until brown on both sides. Drain on blotting paper and serve hot. Serves 4-6.

Humble fresh anchovies or sardines are perhaps my favorite fish, as they are easy to prepare and delicious to eat. They are more often eaten in Mediterranean countries, but I could not resist writing about them in case you ever come across them or their relatives. To clean them, slit the belly open with a knife or your hands, and pull the head off together with the central bone. If you find it easier, cut the head off first and then discard the bone. Open them butterfly-like and carefully wash under running cold water. Set aside to drain in a colander or on blotting paper. At this stage you can do one of three things: (a) coat the fish in flour and fry in olive oil until crisp and brown, (b) sprinkle the fish with olive oil, crushed garlic, and salt, and place under a hot oven grill for about 10-15 minutes, or (c) stuff them as follows:

Stuffed Fresh Anchovies or Sardines

1 cup breadcrumbs, or bread first soaked
  in water then squeezed dry
1 cup grated Romano cheese
1/3 cup chopped parsley
6-8 cloves crushed garlic
3 eggs

2 tablespoons capers
2 tablespoons oregano or dry rosemary,
  finely chopped
flour to coat
oil for frying
2 tablespoons fresh lemon juice

Prepare the fish as described above. In a bowl, combine one egg with the breadcrumbs, cheese, parsley, garlic, capers, and herbs. Mix well. Spread the fish open and cover with about one teaspoon of this mixture; cover with another fish and press it down, patting it flat with the palm of your hands. You can use one or two toothpicks to keep the filling in. Separately, beat two eggs together with the lemon juice. Coat the fish first in egg, then in flour, and fry in hot oil until golden brown and crisp. Serve with lemon wedges. For 24-30 fish.

Variations on Mayonnaise

Mayonnaise

2 egg yolks
$^1/_2$ cup lemon juice
salt and pepper to taste
1 or 1 $^1/_2$ cups olive oil, according to taste
   or to the quantity you need

Separate both egg yolks and whip vigorously with a little salt and pepper until they become pale and fluffy. Add olive oil drop by drop, whipping well all the time until each drop is well absorbed. As the sauce thickens, you can add the oil a little more generously, alternating with a few drops of lemon juice or wine vinegar. Stir constantly until you have the right consistency, bearing in mind that oil thickens and that lemon or vinegar dilute the sauce. Lemon has a delicate flavour and is suitable for accompanying fish; vinegar goes well with salads, vegetables, or chicken.

If you have bad luck making mayonnaise, a foolproof trick is to add a mashed boiled potato to the eggs at the start of the process.

Sauce tartare

A basic mayonnaise to which you add capers, finely chopped chives, finely chopped gherkins, finely-chopped parsley, or any pickled vegetable, finely chopped.

Aioli

Mayonnaise mixed with as much crushed garlic as you think will suit your guests.

Herb mayonnaise

Add finely chopped herbs of your choice to the mayonnaise — use any of the following: fennel, dill, basil, mint, tarragon, fresh oregano, chives. If you want a pink mayonnaise, you can add chopped, boiled red beetroot to it.

Cocktail sauce

Accompanies fish very well. To 1 cup of mayonnaise add 1 teaspoon of Worcestershire sauce, 1 tablespoon of ketchup, 1 tablespoon cognac, 1 tablespoon Dijon mustard, 1 teaspoon sugar, and abundant black pepper.

Saffron mayonnaise

Dissolve $^1/_2$ teaspoon of saffron in 1 to 2 tablespoons of hot water, and let this steep for 2 hours. Drain, then add it to 1 cup of mayonnaise.

Horseradish mayonnaise

Add 1 heaping tablespoon of horseradish sauce to 1 cup of mayonnaise.

You can choose any fish or shellfish you like, depending on what you find at the market. Here is an example:

Platter of Seafood

—*one fairly large fish, such as sea bass, salmon, bream, or fresh cod (about 2 or 3 lb), boiled or grilled, served whole or filleted*
—*fresh, shucked oysters (about 2 per person)*
—*boiled mussels in their half-shell (about 2 per person)*
—*tiger prawns (2 or 3 per person), lightly boiled or grilled*
—*crab or lobster (one large crab or lobster will do for about 6 people), boiled, shelled, and cut into small bits*
—*inkfish (about 1 per person), cleaned, boiled, and cut into small bits*

Place on serving dishes and decorate. For example, use lettuce, lemon slices, tomato slices, black olives, arugula, parsley or bunches of any fresh herbs, strips of yellow, red, or green bell peppers, and so on. Place bowls of different mayonnaises in the centre of the table, so that your guests can try all of them. Aioli (page 31) or Skordaliá (page 33) would also be perfect.

Fresh fowl for our menu was always at hand.

Chicken

The time (and economy) conscious person can organize chicken in such a way as to prepare several meals at once. If you have a freezer, buy two chickens and proceed as follows:

—Remove the breasts (as for "Chicken Breast Pané," page 40). You will have four portions to be used immediately or stored in the freezer.

—Cut off the legs and divide in half. Do the same with the wings. Snip the very tip of the wings and set aside for stock. This will provide you with four to six more portions of chicken that you can cook according to any recipe you like. If not needed immediately, store in the freezer.

—Put the livers aside to use for paté or Crostini. Two livers are enough to make a little paté. A small quantity goes a long way, and it lasts well in the fridge; you can use it for snacks with fresh crusty bread or toast.

—Use the carcass, neck, and the wing tips for stock, with the addition of an onion, a little potato, a few carrots, a couple of bay leaves, a stalk of celery, and herbs. Boil until the meat comes off easily from the bones. This stock can be used for many delicious soups or stored in the freezer for further use. Of course, you can also use it for cooking.

—Retrieve the meat from the boiled bones; you will be surprised to see the amount. Process it in the food processor and set aside for stuffing, chicken balls, or paté. Leave the best bits whole if you want to use them for chicken salad or pie.

A simple recipe that pleased many of our customers — whether English, Italian, or Greek. These chicken breasts can be prepared in advance and refrigerated or frozen until needed.

Chicken Breasts Pané

4 boneless, skinless chicken breasts
flour to coat (about 1 cup)
dry breadcrumbs to coat (about 1 cup)
1 tablespoon fresh lemon juice, or
  2 tablespoons milk

- 1 egg
- 2 tablespoons butter
- 5-6 tablespoons olive oil
- salt to taste
- lemon wedges to decorate

    Place each breast between two sheets of plastic (an ordinary plastic bag will do). Don't use saran wrap or parchment paper, as it breaks easily. Little bits of plastic or paper get embedded in the chicken and have to be picked out one by one, and you have to start all over again.

    Pound with the flat side of a meat mallet to flatten each breast. Coat first in flour, then in the egg beaten with the lemon or milk, and finally in fine breadcrumbs. Press firmly with the palm of your hands until the meat is well covered. Place on a clean plate, covering each piece with cling-wrap or greaseproof paper, and refrigerate until ready to use. Cook in a large skillet with oil and butter on moderate heat until golden brown and thoroughly cooked inside. Sprinkle with salt and serve with lemon wedges. Serves 4.

In Canada I found a delicious and colourful cranberry vinegar with the cranberries bottled in. I use it often and always add a few of the little pickled red fruits in both meat dishes and salads. This popular Italian chicken dish is usually cooked with dry white wine or vinegar, or a little cognac, and wild mushrooms.

Chicken alla Cacciatora

1 medium-sized chicken (about 3 ¹/₂ lb), chopped into chunks
flour to coat
6 tablespoons olive oil
2 tablespoons butter
4 crushed garlic cloves
1 tablespoon finely chopped rosemary, fresh or dry
¹/₃ cup cranberry vinegar

2 cups chicken broth
1 cup or more finely sliced mushrooms, according to your taste (wild, oyster, Portobello, or button mushrooms)
¹/₄ cup finely chopped fresh parsley
salt and freshly ground black pepper
1 tablespoon flour for the roux
1 tablespoon butter

Coat the chicken in flour. Heat the oil and 2 tablespoons butter in a large, heavy skillet over medium-high heat. Sauté the chicken until brown on all sides. Remove the chicken and set it aside, along with the browned bits scraped carefully from the bottom of the pan. In a clean pan or casserole, sauté the garlic until it colours. Stir in the rosemary, vinegar and cranberries (if using). Bring to a simmer, and return the chicken to the pan along with the scraped bits and the broth. Reduce the heat and let it simmer until the chicken is thoroughly cooked (about 20-25 minutes). Prepare the roux using 1 tablespoon of flour and one tablespoon of butter. Dissolve the roux well in a little cold water or wine and add to the casserole, stirring often for a few more minutes. Meanwhile, in another pan, sauté the mushrooms with a few drops of olive oil until browned. Add to the chicken, season with salt and pepper, and sprinkle with the chopped parsley. Serve with rice or mashed potatoes. If you are not a purist, you can use a package of dried asparagus or mushroom soup instead of making the roux. Dissolve in cold milk or broth and add to the casserole; it will make a very tasty sauce.

This is a wonderfully spiced curry for those who like it hot. Serve it with steaming boiled rice and a selection of side dishes such as fried onions, peanuts, chopped bananas sprinkled with lemon juice, pineapple chunks, cucumber, etc.

Chicken Indian Style

1 medium-sized chicken (about 2 ¹/₂ lb) chopped in chunks
1 cup flour
1 cup finely chopped almonds or hazelnuts
1 generous pinch each of cumin, cardamom, cinnamon, coriander, and dried lemongrass
2 tablespoons finely chopped fresh ginger
6 tablespoons olive oil
1 tablespoon butter

2-3 fresh or dried chili peppers whole (or chopped finely if you like it very hot)
1 shallot, chopped finely
6 crushed cloves of garlic
1 cup chicken broth or coconut milk
2 cups tomato juice
1 teaspoon grated lemon zest
1 cup plain yogurt
salt to taste

In a large bowl, combine the flour, chopped nuts, and dried spices. Dip the chicken in this mixture, pressing it in well to coat on all sides.

Heat the olive oil and butter in a large, heavy-bottomed skillet, and sauté the shallot, chili, garlic, and ginger. Add the chicken and cook until well browned, stirring frequently. Add the broth or milk, and simmer until the chicken is very tender. Stir in the tomato juice, lemon zest, and salt and keep simmering a few more minutes. Just before serving, add the yogurt, stir again, and serve piping hot. Serves 6.

The combination of green peppers, tomato sauce, and white rice makes this dish colourful as well as very tasty.

Chicken alla Romana

1 medium-sized chicken (about 3 1/2 lb)	1 fresh chili pepper (optional)
6 tablespoons olive oil	2 1/2 cups tomato juice
1 onion, chopped finely	salt and pepper to taste
5-6 green bell peppers	2 tablespoons oil to braise the vegetables

Cut the chicken into small portions or chunks. Heat the oil in a large, heavy pan over medium-high heat, and brown the chicken well all round. Reduce the heat, cover with a lid, and simmer until the chicken is tender. Set it aside and scrape the browned bits from the bottom of the pan, saving these together with the chicken. Wipe the pan clean. Sauté the onion, peppers, and chili with 2 tablespoons olive oil until softened. Return the chicken to the pan with the vegetables, add the tomato juice, salt, and pepper, and simmer for another few minutes until the sauce is slightly thickened. If you like it hot, you can chop the chili pepper with seeds and all; otherwise, leave it whole and simply discard it when the sauce is ready. Serves 6-8.

Meat

✤

The way an animal is treated and fed makes a great difference in the taste. Of course few of us, like Nero Wolfe, can order pigs to be fattened on blueberries; at most, if you are lucky enough, you may find a free-range chicken. Poor pigs nowadays are not even allowed to get fat, in order to keep our precious human cholesterol low. Without fat, though, pork or any other meat does not taste half as good. If you buy prosciutto, choose one with a good layer of lard and you'll see the difference. Personally I think one can live very well on salads and pasta, but if one has a full meal, it might as well be good!

I find meat is excellent in Nova Scotia, especially beef. Most lamb is imported frozen, and cannot compare with a fresh lamb or kid, fed on milk or on good old-fashioned grass, and roasted with herbs to perfection. Chicken, pork, and lamb should always be thoroughly cooked—not

only for your health, but for the taste. Rare lamb, in particular, tastes slightly of live, unwashed sheep.

I find that these days we have to use more herbs and spices as we deal with less genuine products. Don't be afraid of adding an extra pinch or marjoram or an extra clove of garlic— God knows I have done it often enough and nobody ever complained. Use marinades freely, and invent your own. You can choose from innumerable ingredients such as olive oil, lemon juice or vinegar, wine, liqueurs, orange and lemon zest, orange juice, beer, fresh or dried herbs, spices, garlic, onions, chili pepper, mustard, peanut butter, anchovy paste, even a little honey or sugar (especially for pork or chicken). You'll have fun creating your own recipes. Don't mix too many ingredients at a time— except in Oriental cooking—but do try new ones often.

◀ *We rented a charming old Venetian villa.*

This dish comes from Milan and is prepared with thin slices of veal (as for scaloppine). Veal chops may be used if they are not cut too thick, in which case you will have to bone and trim the meat, and flatten it well with the side of a mallet.

Frittura Piccata

*8-10 veal scaloppine or 4 veal chops
    (pounded flat)
3 tablespoons butter
3-4 tablespoons olive oil
flour to coat*

*2 cups hot stock (chicken or beef; if you bone
    the chops, you can use the bones for stock)
fresh lemon juice (half a lemon or more
    according to your taste)
2 tablespoons fresh chopped parsley
salt to taste*

Coat the veal in the flour, pressing it well with the palms of your hands. Heat oil and butter in a heavy pan and sauté the veal on medium fire until very lightly brown on both sides. Set the meat aside. Pour the stock in the pan, and stir well to loosen all the bits from the bottom. Return the meat to the pan, making sure there is enough liquid to cover it. Turn the heat down, cover the pan with a lid, and simmer until the meat is tender. Stir often and, if necessary, add a little more broth or water to avoid sticking. Sprinkle with salt, lemon juice, and parsley. Simmer for another minute or two and serve hot. Mashed potatoes accompany this dish very well. Serves 4.

From the Italian stufato (slowly braised over a stufa, or stove) this dish was brought to Corfu by the Venetians. Stifado is found nowhere in Greece except for Corfu, where it evolved into a really interesting sweet-and-sour dish.

Stifado

2-2 ¹/₂ lb rump roast
6 tablespoons olive oil
6 dozen baby onions, or about 12 small
   onions

2 teaspoons sugar or honey
¹/₂ cup red wine vinegar
2 cups tomato juice
salt to taste and abundant black pepper

Heat the oil in a large, heavy casserole, and brown the meat all over on lively heat. Lower the heat to minimum, cover the casserole, and simmer until the meat is thoroughly cooked and the liquid evaporated. Add the onions and honey or sugar, and stir often until brown and caramelized. (Baby onions, as you know, are a pain to peel. If time or patience are short, substitute with ordinary red onions, as small as possible.) Add the vinegar and let it evaporate for a minute or so, then add the tomato juice, salt, and pepper. Let it simmer until the sauce thickens slightly, and serve hot. In Corfu they sometimes add a few cloves, but I prefer it without. Boiled rice is a good accompaniment to this dish. Serves 6.

The Venetian Safe

❦ This was one of the many little miracles
that happened in our restaurant. We were near
opening night, very near the end of our money and
we still had to buy a refrigerator — obviously vital
for a restaurant. Luckily my husband Stephanos
knew of a butcher's shop that went bust, and the
owner wanted to sell his large and almost new
refrigerator. We went together to his shop, which
was rather a mess, as it was to be re-converted.
Much of the equipment was in the way. While my
husband and the butcher negotiated, my eye fell on

Work at times was staggering.

a beautiful old iron safe, all spluttered with paint and piled up in a corner with other stuff. It must
have been from the sixteenth century, when the Venetians were in Corfu, and I loved it at first
sight. I kept interrupting the two men until they both grew so annoyed with me it was practically
given to me, for next to nothing, so long as I shut up. It arrived the next day at our restaurant,
together with the fridge. After days of scrubbing and polishing, it became a great piece of attraction.
Very soon afterwards, an antique dealer from Amsterdam saw it, bought it, and had it sent home
by plane. I hated to see it go, but we were able to buy a few things that were needed.

This is the Corfiote version of the previous recipe. It is less delicate but still a very

tasty dish. You can use either beef or veal, thinly sliced and tender.

Soffritto

6 veal chops or 6 beef slices, well pounded	*¹/₃ cup red wine vinegar*
flour to coat	*salt and pepper to taste*
6 cloves of crushed garlic	*2 tablespoons parsley, finely chopped*
2 cups broth or water	*6 + 1 tablespoons olive oil*

Coat the meat in flour, pressing it well with the palms of your hands. Heat the oil in a large, heavy skillet, reserving one tablespoon. Sauté on medium heat until lightly brown on both sides. Remove the meat and set aside. Add a little broth to the pan, and stir well to detach all the bits in the bottom. Set this aside with the meat. Wipe the pan clean and sauté the garlic with one tablespoon olive oil. As soon as it starts to colour, add the vinegar. After a minute or two, add the rest of the broth and the meat. Simmer on low fire, topped with a lid, until the meat is very tender. Stir frequently to avoid sticking, and add more liquid if necessary (broth or water). Season with salt and pepper, stir a few moments until it dissolves, and serve hot. Serves 6.

There are many cuts of meat suitable for this dish. Eye of round cuts beautifully and presents a more elegant dish for a party, but less expensive cuts like brisket or shank are tasty. In Milan, restaurants often offer a selection of boiled meats with this sauce, such as beef, veal, tongue, and chicken. Whichever you choose, make sure you boil the meat until it is so tender that it can be cut with a fork. The Sauce Piquante is also good with boiled inkfish or shellfish.

Boiled Beef with Sauce Piquante

Sauce Piquante
1 heaping tablespoon chopped fresh parsley
2 tablespoons capers
1 heaping teaspoon prepared Dijon mustard
1 heaping teaspoon anchovy paste
1/4 cup red wine vinegar
1/2 cup virgin olive oil
2-3 crushed garlic cloves
salt and pepper to taste

1 large onion
1 carrot
1 stalk of celery
1-2 bay leaves

1 sprig of fresh thyme
1 teaspoon whole black peppercorns
salt to taste
beef of your choice

Place the meat in a pot of *boiling* water, with the onion, carrot, celery, herbs, and pepper. Make sure there is enough water to cover the meat. Lower the heat and simmer until very tender, adding the salt only toward the end, as it tends to toughen the meat. Serve hot with sauce piquante. Serves 6.

If you prefer, garlic can be replaced by finely chopped spring onions or chives. Mix all the ingredients together, and add vinegar a little at a time to suit your taste, as some are stronger than others.

Ask your butcher for 6 portions of the cut of your choice, as quantities vary according to cuts; he or she will advise you.

Ossobuco means "bone with a hole." It is a thick slice of meat with a central bone, cut from the shank of veal or beef. When cooked long and slowly, the marrow melts, creating a mouthwatering flavor. Traditionally it is served in Milan (where it originated) with saffron risotto, but it is also excellent with mashed potatoes, buttered rice, or polenta.

Ossobuco

4 beef or veal shank slices
6 tablespoons olive oil
3 tablespoons butter
1 large onion, finely chopped
2 carrots, finely chopped
2 celery stalks, finely sliced
2 crushed garlic cloves
1 cup dry white wine

1 1/2 cups tomato juice
1 bay leaf
2 tablespoons fresh parsley, chopped
2 tablespoons finely chopped dry rosemary
2 teaspoons lemon zest
1-2 cups stock
salt and freshly ground black pepper
1 heaping teaspoon flour

Heat the olive oil and butter in a large, heavy pan or casserole. Brown the meat all over—in batches if necessary—then remove and set aside. Sauté onions, carrots, and celery in the same casserole until the onion is soft and translucent. Add the garlic and all herbs except the parsley. After a minute or two, return the meat to the casserole, sprinkle with the flour, and stir well. Add the wine and simmer for a minute or two, then stir in the tomato juice, salt, and pepper, and enough stock to keep the meat just covered. Bring to a boil, then lower the heat, cover the casserole, and simmer very slowly until the meat is so tender that it falls from the bone. Stir frequently to avoid sticking, and if necessary add more stock or water, a little at a time. At the last moment, sprinkle with lemon zest and parsley; give it a few more moments and serve hot. Serves 4.

Polenta is treated here as a main dish because it is usually served with meat (beef, veal, pork, sausages, chicken, and in some parts of Italy even fish) —and also because it is very filling. Polenta is extremely versatile. It can be served plain with melted butter and Parmesan cheese, or with tomato sauce and cheese. Leftovers can be shaped into rounds or squares and grilled to accompany meat. In the Italian Alps, polenta is often eaten for breakfast, either cold with hot milk, or vice versa; the milk itself often fresh from the cow. It can even be used for desserts, although they tend to be heavy. Polenta can be cooked in salted water or milk, or half and half of each. The traditional way of cooking polenta is slow and rather tiring, as one has to stir it all the time, and that is probably why many people don't cook it very often. My own method has many advantages: you can prepare it well in advance, you won't get tired, you won't have any lumps in the polenta, and it will not stick to the bottom as it invariably does when cooked the traditional way.

Polenta with Ragout

1 cup cornmeal
4 1/3 cups cold milk
2 heaping tablespoons butter

salt to taste
3/4 cup freshly grated Parmesan cheese

Dissolve one cup of coarse-grained cornmeal (the organic one is particularly tasty) in the cold milk. Add salt to taste and bring to a boil, stirring constantly with a wooden spoon. When it really bubbles, turn off the heat completely, cover with a lid, and leave it alone. It will keep cooking on its own for quite some time, especially if you have an electric cooker, which takes long to cool. In your own good time—you should wait at least 10 minutes—go back to your polenta and repeat this process. After two or three times, at most, the cornmeal no longer tastes raw and the polenta is well cooked. Remember that if it is too thick, you can add more hot liquid; if too liquid, just cook a few more minutes with the lid off to let the liquid evaporate. Just before serving, stir in the butter, abundant Parmesan cheese, and serve with Ragout (see recipe on the following page), or with the meat or sauce of your choice. Serves 6-8.

Oxtail, shank, or brisket are good for this recipe, although you can use any meat you like – veal, beef, or pork.

Salt and tomatoes (or tomato juice) toughen the meat, and should always be added toward the end of your cooking.

Ragout

2 lb meat of your choice	6 tablespoons olive oil
1 large chopped onion	1 tablespoon butter
1 celery stalk, sliced	salt to taste
1 sliced carrot	black pepper or dry chili pepper to taste
1 teaspoon dry oregano or thyme	2 cups tomato juice
1 teaspoon dry rosemary, chopped finely	2 cloves crushed garlic
flour to coat	1 cup sliced and sautéed mushrooms,
1-1 ½ cups stock, or dry white wine,	optional
or water	

Cut the meat in cubes and coat in flour. Heat the oil and butter in a large, heavy casserole and sauté the onion, carrot, celery, and chili with the herbs. When the onion becomes translucent, add the garlic and keep simmering for a minute or two. With a slotted spoon, remove the vegetables from the casserole, leaving as much oil as possible in the pan, and set aside. Add the meat and cook on medium heat until browned all over, stirring frequently to avoid sticking. Turn the heat down, return the vegetables to the casserole with the meat, and add the stock. Simmer with the lid on until the meat is very tender. If necessary, add more liquid, a little at a time, as required. Last of all, add the tomato juice, along with salt and pepper to taste. Simmer for a few minutes until the sauce thickens. A cup of sliced mushrooms, fried with garlic and parsley, can be added to make the sauce even richer. Serves 6-8.

Kumquats are tiny, oval, bitter, bright orange citrus fruit. In Corfu they are commonly grown and made into candied fruit and a liqueur that's far too sweet to drink — but delicious for cooking. Its sweet-bitter taste goes very well with pork or chicken. I substituted Cointreau and orange zest for Kumquat liqueur, which is not easily found in Canada.

Roast Pork with Kumquat

2 lb pork loin or 4 pork chops
1 tablespoon butter
2-3 tablespoons olive oil
1/3 cup Cointreau
1 teaspoon honey or sugar

salt and black pepper to taste
1 tablespoon orange zest
2-3 tablespoons white wine or orange juice
1 teaspoon cornflour stirred in 1/2 cup water

Sauté the meat on high heat with the oil and butter, until browned all over. Reduce the heat, cover the casserole with a lid, and keep simmering until thoroughly cooked. Uncover the casserole and add the Cointreau, sugar or honey, salt and pepper, and orange zest. Stir until the liquid is slightly reduced and caramelized, adding the wine or orange juice a little at a time as it evaporates. For a thicker sauce, add the cornflour—well stirred in cold water—and simmer five minutes more. Serves 4.

Aliki

When we could finally afford to have somebody come to help us, we were lucky enough to find Aliki. Aliki had seventeen children and lived at that time in one large basement room, without a bathroom and without water. They used a little shack of a toilet and a water tap that were both in the courtyard. Her husband had a motor tricycle that spluttered evil black smoke, which he used for small transport. Aliki washed, fed, and sent her children to school in the morning, cleaned her quarters, and helped her husband carry things for transport. She then fed her family again, put her children to bed and in the evening, she came to help me with the cleaning and washing up. I never saw her without a smile on her face, even when her husband drank and beat her, in which case she always covered up and made excuses for him. Every time I was dropping off with fatigue, I would think of Aliki and feel ashamed of myself. She won't read this book as she never went to school, but wherever you are, God bless you and thank you, Aliki.

Supplies came to us along narrow, tree-lined roads.

This recipe works equally well for pork chops, veal chops, or chicken.

Chops in Cranberry Vinegar

6 pork chops (or veal chops, or six
   portions of chicken with the skin on)
4 tablespoons olive oil
1 tablespoon butter
6 cloves of garlic, crushed
1 ¹/₂ tablespoons finely chopped ginger

1 tablespoon Dijon mustard
¹/₂ cup cranberry vinegar, preferably the
   kind with the berries in it
salt and pepper to taste
1 tablespoon flour
1 cup stock or water

    Pound the chops with the side of the mallet, trying to flatten them without
breaking the bone. Sauté on medium heat with the butter and oil, until brown
on both sides. Remove and set aside. In the same pan, fry the garlic and ginger
until the garlic starts to colour. Add the mustard and vinegar (with a few cranberries, if available) and stir well. Return the meat to the pan, season it with salt
and pepper, and cover with a lid. Simmer until the meat is thoroughly cooked
and tender, stirring often. Add a little hot water or broth if needed to prevent
the meat from sticking. While the meat is simmering, whisk together a cup of
cold water or stock with the flour, add it to the pan, and simmer for a minute or
two until the sauce thickens. Serves 6.

Babel

✣ Talking to our clients was hardly ever a problem, as most of them spoke English, or Greek, or Italian. Only occasionally were there exceptions, almost always with Scandinavians. About 99 percent of them spoke perfect English; when they did not, we resorted to the traditional Greek habit of taking people to the kitchen and letting them choose by pointing their fingers. Once we were quite busy and I was helping to serve the tables. A couple had finished eating and, just before taking away their dishes, I asked, "Finish?" "No, Swedish," the husband told me with a big smile.

All the chicken in Corfu were "free-range."

At Easter time, every family in Greece will grill a lamb on the spit, over a bed of charcoal. If they don't have a yard or a garden, they'll join a relative who has. A little dish with olive oil and lemon juice is placed near the spit, and a branch of rosemary is dipped in it to brush the lamb from time to time.

Marinated Lamb Chops

8-10 lamb chops
2 tablespoons maple syrup or honey
4 garlic cloves, crushed
2 tablespoons fresh or dried rosemary,
   finely chopped
3 tablespoons wine vinegar
2 tablespoons olive oil

1 teaspoon grated lemon zest
1 large egg or 2 medium eggs
salt and pepper to taste
flour to coat
breadcrumbs to coat
olive oil for frying (about
   6 tablespoons)

Cut off the fatty skin and flatten the chops with a mallet. If you splinter the bone during this process, make sure that no splinters are left in the meat. Prepare a marinade with the oil, vinegar, honey, garlic, rosemary, lemon zest, salt, and pepper. Leave the chops in the marinade overnight.

Coat the lamb chops in the flour, then in the beaten egg, and finally in the breadcrumbs. Press the chops well into the breadcrumbs, flattening them with the palm of your hand. Heat the olive oil in a large skillet and fry the meat on both sides, over medium heat, until thoroughly cooked and golden brown. If you serve the lamb with roasted potatoes, drizzle any leftover marinade over the potatoes before roasting them in the oven. Serves 4-5.

I prefer the taste of the shoulder to the leg of lamb, but you can use either one.

Roasted Lamb Shoulder

6 cloves of garlic, crushed
3 tablespoons chopped fresh apple-mint
3 tablespoons dried thyme
3 tablespoons cognac
shoulder of lamb, 6 or 7 lb

1 tablespoon olive oil
1 tablespoon butter
1 tablespoon flour
salt and pepper to taste

Prepare a paste with the garlic, herbs, and cognac. Pierce the meat with a pointed knife in several places to make slits of about 1 inch. Insert the herb paste into each slit, pressing it down well. Rub the meat with the olive oil and the butter, then sprinkle it with the flour, salt, and pepper, rubbing this in with your fingertips. Place the meat in a roasting pan and preheat the oven to 400°F. When the meat has rested for at least 20 minutes and the oven is very hot, place the meat inside and let cook until it starts to brown. At this point, turn the oven down to 350°F. Continue to cook until the meat is thoroughly brown and tender. Check often to make sure the outside crust doesn't burn (if necessary, cover with a sheet of aluminum foil). Serves 6-8.

Desserts

In Corfu we had a variety of magnificent fruit. Tourists coming from the North would sit almost mesmerized under our vine pergola. Vines grew everywhere and often escaped from the vineyard to climb up the tall cypresses, maybe intertwined with dog-roses or wisteria. Lemon and orange trees were also greatly admired, as in those days one did not travel so much, and many tourists had never seen an orange tree before. One of our friends, a lovely English boy who acted as a guide in summer, took a group of people through an orange grove, and an English lady asked him what oranges were used for? "Orange oil," he replied coolly.

Figs thrive in the island, and a great quantity are dried in the sun, chopped, and mixed with Raki (a potent anise-flavored drink, similar to grappa), pepper, and spices, and then wrapped in chestnut leaves. These compact little cakes (sikópites) keep for months, and in winter a thin slice of sikópita with a glass of wine in front of the fireplace is a very good idea. As to fresh figs, there is a great difference between one just picked from the tree, with its honey drop at one end, and one imported from the other end of the world. About the same difference between me and Sophia Loren. Melons and peaches of many kinds grow in summer. Perhaps the best is a very perfumed green peach with a white-pink pulp. The peasants run a sharp knife through a lemon (with the rind on) before finely slicing these peaches. This by itself is a kingly dessert.

◀ *Masses of wildflowers covered the whole island.*

This is a fabulous dessert, which is both mouthwatering and simple. Triona is an Irish friend of mine, who first made it for me.

Gâteau Diane à la Triona

1 teaspoon cornstarch
1 teaspoon vinegar
5 eggs
10 ounces sugar

200-gram bar of milk chocolate
2 pints cream
2 teaspoons vanilla

Pavlova

The meringue prepared as above can also be used to make a Pavlova. For this dessert, you spread spoonfuls of meringue to form a single, round layer. Bake in the same manner described above, and top with fresh whipped cream and the fruit of your choice. A little lemon zest added to the cream gives it a delicious flavor.

Separate five eggs, saving the yolks for custard or mayonnaise. Whip the whites into stiff peaks. When whites are dry and shiny, pour in half of the sugar, a little at a time, then add the vanilla, cornstarch, and vinegar. Preheat your oven to 300°F. Fold in gently the rest of the sugar and pour the mixture into a rectangular cookie tin, well greased and covered with tinfoil. Cook for an hour, then turn the oven off and let it rest for about 10-15 minutes with the oven door ajar. Cut the meringue into three even rectangles, allowing them to dry away from draughts. Place the first rectangle on a serving dish. Cover it with chocolate cream, then add the next layers, spreading lots of cream on each one. Last, using a spatula, cover the top and sides with the remaining cream. Decorate with shaved or grated chocolate.

Chocolate cream: whip the cream until it is stiff. Gently fold in 150 grams of chocolate previously melted in a double boiler or microwave (be careful not to cook it too long in the microwave, as it burns easily and would then be useless). If the chocolate is warm, it sometimes hardens, giving a nice chocolate crunch to the cream. You can vary the taste by using dark chocolate, but milk chocolate works well. Grate the remaining 50 grams of chocolate over your gâteau. Serves 8.

This dessert means "milk pie" in Greek, though is probably of Turkish origin. It can be eaten hot or cold.

Galattópita

1 cup semolina
3 cups cold milk
4 tablespoons sugar
1 teaspoon lemon zest
1/2 teaspoon salt
4 tablespoons melted butter

2 eggs, beaten
6 sheets frozen phyllo pastry, thawed
1/4 cup maple syrup
1/2 cup breadcrumbs and/or nuts
   (almonds, walnuts, or hazelnuts)

Apple Pie with Phyllo

You can actually use any fruit you like for these phyllo pies; for example, pears, apricots, peaches, figs, or pineapple. If the fruit is very juicy, sprinkle it with a little cornflour before using it. Use about one tablespoon of sugar for every cup of fruit. These pies are good when hot or cold, and can be served with whipped cream, custard, or ice cream.

Assemble the ingredients and proceed as in the previous recipe; substitute the semolina filling with 3 cups of the fruit of your choice.

Preheat the oven to 325°F. Combine the cold milk, semolina, lemon zest, and 2 tablespoons of sugar in a saucepan. Bring to a boil, then turn the heat to low and simmer for about 10 minutes, stirring constantly. Remove from the heat and set aside. Stir in half of the butter. Line a greased backing dish (about 10-12 inches) with 2 sheets of phyllo, and brush with some of the remaining butter. Sprinkle with sugar and breadcrumbs. Instead of breadcrumbs, you could also use finely crushed nuts of your choice. Add 2 more sheets of phyllo and sprinkle again with the sugar and the breadcrumbs or nuts.

Beat the eggs together and stir in the semolina, setting aside 1 tablespoon of the beateb egg. Pour into the baking dish. Fold the overhanging pastry edges into the centre of the baking dish. Cover with the remaining 2 sheets of phyllo, again brush with butter, sugar, and breadcrumbs. This time tuck the edges under themselves to make a tidy edge. Brush the top with the leftover egg. Bake for 20-25 minutes until golden brown. Remove from the oven, drizzle the maple syrup on top, and allow the pie to cool slightly before serving. Serves 6.

This dessert could not be any simpler and everybody loves it, especially children.

Apple Fritters

3 large apples, peeled, cored and finely
  sliced into rounds
vegetable oil for deep frying
powdered sugar to serve

For the batter:
- *1 cup flour*
- *2 eggs, separated*
- *a splash of brandy*
- *a pinch of salt*
- *¹/₂ cup water*
- *¹/₂ teaspoon baking powder*

Peel, core, and slice the apples into rounds, as thinly as possible, sprinkling them with a few drops of lemon juice to prevent discolouring. Dip each slice in batter and deep-fry in hot vegetable oil on both sides. Sprinkle with powdered sugar and serve hot. For batter, you can use the recipe on page 8, or the one given above: whisk together the flour, brandy, egg yolks, a pinch of salt, ¹/₂ cup of water, and ¹/₂ teaspoon baking powder. Fold in the stiffly beaten egg whites. Serves 4-6.

Fried Eggs

A sweet dish for those occasions when a quick family dessert is needed and you have no time, or as a special treat for a child. Pour a generous dollop of whipped cream in each individual dish, place a tinned half peach round side up in the centre of the cream, and sprinkle with cocoa or cinnamon to imitate pepper. You have created oeuf-au-plat, which is fun for all and might fool the very youngest! In our restaurant we even fooled, for a moment, a grown-up or two.

Best made in spring, when almonds are fresh and tasty. It's my version of the centuries-old blancmange, and can be prepared well in advance, or the day before you need it.

Almond Cream

4 eggs, separated
4 tablespoons sugar
1 heaping teaspoon cornstarch
1 cup ground almonds
2 cups milk

1 packet unflavored gelatin
whipped cream and slivered almonds
  to serve
1 tablespoon almond extract or vanilla

Make sure to use very fresh farm eggs. Whisk yolks with the sugar and cornflour until white and fluffy. Add the almond extract if it is of very good quality; if not, use vanilla. Pour in the milk, a little at a time. Cook on moderate heat until the cream thickens and coats the spoon, stirring all the while. Take off the heat.

Next, dissolve one packet of unflavored gelatin in half a cup of boiling water, then stir in another half cup of cold water. Wait until the gelatin is completely dissolved before stirring it into the cooling almond cream. Mix thoroughly. Whip the egg whites until firm and stiff, and fold them gently into the mixture. Pour into a well-buttered mould and chill for a few hours or overnight. Unmould and serve with whipped cream, along with plain or caramelized almond slivers. (You can either toast these slivers lightly in a pan, or caramelize them by tossing a little sugar in the pan until they are golden brown). Serves 6.

Simple, delicious, and you can prepare it well in advance.

While this recipe can be used with other fruit, it's particularly good with pears.

Pears in Wine

6 large pears, not over-ripe
sugar to taste
red wine
the rind of half a lemon

4 tablespoons of ripe, fresh raspberries, or
strawberries, or cranberries
whipped cream or vanilla ice cream to serve

Peel the pears, leaving the stalk intact. Slightly pare their bottoms so they can stand up in a casserole dish, which should just be big enough to accommodate them. Add enough red wine to half-cover the fruit, then add the lemon rind, sugar to taste, and the raspberries. Simmer with a lid on until the pears are tender and easily pierced with a fork. Remove the pears carefully and place them on a serving dish. Leave the juice to simmer until dense and syrupy. Pour on the pears and insert a bay leaf or a leaf of mint next to the stalk for decoration. Serve cold or lukewarm with whipped cream, custard, or ice cream. Serves 6.

Micetta and the Mice

In summer, when everybody naturally likes to eat in the garden, Corfu invariably attracts a number of mice. Gerald Durrell told us they are a special fruit-eating race, and are not related to rats. It's true enough that they kept to trees and never came inside, but I still worried about them. We had several fruit trees that attracted them, particularly a huge palm tree with little orange-coloured fruit they seemed to love. The traffic and noise of tourists eventually got rid of them, but at the beginning we had to keep a cat or two on the premises. One of them is probably remembered by a number of our clients, a charming lady-cat called Micetta. Her true vocation was not chasing mice — she was far too ladylike — but nursing. If you coughed or sneezed, she would rush at you in a flash, put her front paws round your neck, and look anxiously at your eyes. We tried to warn people and keep the cat locked up, but at busy times we would forget and a few of our clients were quite startled by this treatment. Luckily, they were all very nice about it and often came back for more nursing.

Fruit was always on the menu.

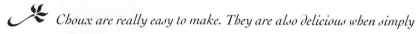 *Choux are really easy to make. They are also delicious when simply filled with whipped cream and accompanied by fresh strawberries.*

Choux with Zabaglione

For the choux pastry:
1 cup water
½ cup butter
a pinch of salt
For the zabaglione:
4 egg yolks
4 tablespoons sugar
½ cup marsala (or sherry, or port)

Or, in place of the zabaglione, you may substitute custard:
4 egg yolks
1 teaspoon cornflour, or 1 tablespoon flour
4 tablespoons sugar
2 cups milk
lemon rind

Choux

To make the choux pastry: put one cup of water, half a cup of butter, and a pinch of salt in a saucepan and bring to a boil. When the butter is melted and the water boiled, add one cup of flour all at once, lower the heat, and stir constantly until the mixture forms a ball and pulls away from the pan. Remove from the heat and add three eggs, one at a time, stirring well after each addition, making sure that each egg is absorbed before adding the next. Shape into walnut-sized balls with two wet teaspoons and place on a buttered and lightly-floured oven tray, spacing the balls about 2 inches apart. Cool in the fridge for an hour or so, then bake in a preheated oven at 400°F for 15 minutes. Lower the oven to 350°F and bake for a further 10-12 minutes. Turn the oven off and leave the choux inside—with the oven door ajar—for a quarter of an hour.   The last step is to cut off the tops of each choux and fill with a mixture of zabaglione and whipped cream (half and half). Sprinkle with icing sugar or drizzle with caramel.

Zabaglione

Whisk four yolks with four tablespoons of sugar until fluffy and lemon-coloured. Place the bowl over a saucepan of simmering water or a double boiler and whip constantly, on moderate heat, until the sauce becomes fluffy and thick. It's only fair to warn you that zabaglione is tricky; I always find it one of the most difficult things to make. Unless I want a golden medal, I substitute it with a simple egg custard and just add the marsala to that.

Egg custard, or crème anglaise

Whisk egg yolks, sugar, and flour in a saucepan until fluffy. Add a rind of lemon and the cold milk. Bring to a slow boil, stirring all the time with a wooden spoon, and remove quickly from the fire as soon as it coats the spoon. Keep stirring for a minute, remove the lemon rind, and add the marsala. Serves 6.

Fresh chestnuts are best for this recipe, if you have the energy and time to boil, cut, peel, and purée them. I find canned chestnut purée an excellent substitute.

Mont Blanc

2 cups chestnut purée, canned or fresh
2 tablespoons cocoa powder
1 heaping tablespoon grated chocolate

¹/₃ cup white rum, kirsch, or cognac sugar
to taste
biscuits of your choice, as needed

Stir the cocoa, chocolate, and liqueur into the chestnut purée, taste for sweetness, and add a little more sugar if needed. On a serving dish, prepare a bed of ladyfingers, savoyards or Millefoglie biscuits, or meringue nests. By using the back of a spoon or a pestle, push the mixture through a sieve over the biscuits, trying to obtain a cone-shaped peak. Top with whipped cream. Makes 2 cups.

Two Easy Desserts

❧

Torciglioni

From the Italian torcere, *"to twist," they can be served with whipped cream or ice cream for a family dessert, or used as tea biscuits.*

frozen puff pastry, thawed   *sugar*
crushed nuts   *butter (quantities as required)*

Preheat the oven to 425°F and lightly butter a cookie sheet. Roll out the pastry on a floured surface until about $1/8$-inch thick. Brush the surface with melted butter, then sprinkle with sugar and finely chopped nuts: almonds, hazelnuts, walnuts, or any other kind. Using the rolling pin, press nuts well into the pastry. Cut into 1-inch-wide strips and twist them gently from end to end, to form spirals. Bake for about 10-12 minutes until puffed and golden brown. Cool on a rack.

Lemon (or Grapefruit) Tart

Light and crunchy, this makes an ideal dessert with a sweet and tart flavor.

frozen puff pastry, thawed, 1 packet   *1 or 2 lemons, finely*
4 tablespoons of sugar   *sliced, or 1 large grape-*
1 tablespoon butter   *fruit, finely sliced*

Preheat the oven to 425°F and lightly butter a shallow baking tin of any shape you like. Roll out the pastry to $1/8$-inch thickness. Line the bottom and sides of the baking tin, and pierce the pastry all over with a fork. Peel off the rind of the lemon or grapefruit, and slice the fruit as thin as possible, getting rid of any pips. Arrange the slices neatly over the pastry, slightly overlapping them (if it is a round tin, start from the centre). Bake for about 10-12 minutes, then reduce heat to 350°F, until the tart is puffed up and golden brown—about 10 more minutes. Meanwhile, put the sugar with 2-3 tablespoons water in a small casserole, and let it bubble till the caramel is golden brown. Take it off the fire and quickly drizzle it over the tart, forming criss-crosses and curlicues. To have a thin drizzle, let it fall on the tart from a spoon or a fork held at a good height.

It can be prepared several hours in advance or the day before you want it. To unmould it easily without any mishaps, you should refrigerate it first for at least two hours, then freeze it for 30-40 minutes. Just before unmoulding, place it in a bowl full of boiling water for a few seconds.

Fruit Charlotte with Custard

3 egg yolks
3 tablespoons sugar
1 teaspoon lemon zest
1 teaspoon cornflour
1 packet unflavored gelatine
2 1/2 cups milk

about 2 packets of Millefoglie or savoyard
    biscuits, or ladyfingers
one 1/2-kilo can of peaches, pears, or
    pineapple
whipped cream and fresh fruit to decorate
2-3 sprigs of mint

Whisk together the yolks, sugar, lemon zest, and cornflour. Add the milk a little at a time, stirring well. Place on medium heat, and keep stirring slowly until the custard thickens and coats the back of your wooden spoon. Take off the heat and cover with a lid. Dissolve the gelatine in half a cup of boiling water, then add another half-cup of cold water, and wait until the gelatine is completely dissolved. Stir well into the custard. Butter a nice bowl or mould and line its bottom and sides with the biscuits of your choice. Drizzle them with the syrup of the canned fruit. Alternate layers of custard, fruit (drained and chopped into pieces), and the syrup-drizzled biscuits, until the mould is full. Prod with the tip of a knife to make sure the custard and syrup reach everywhere. Refrigerate for at least two or three hours. Unmould and decorate with whipped cream. A few fresh strawberries, raspberries, and sprigs of mint will make it very attractive. If children are not going to eat it, you can add a little white rum to the fruit syrup. Serves 6.

The Jacaranda Tree

❧ When the owner of our restaurant decided to demolish it and develop the area, we had to move to another place. The second Nausicaa was not bad, but it lacked the charm of the original one. Twelve blocks of flats, painted a murky mustard yellow, soon rose and replaced our old Venetian villa. And, even worse, all the beautiful trees were destroyed, including our beautiful pepper trees and a magnificent enormous magnolia tree that must have been centuries old. I was able to salvage the trunk of a jacaranda tree that was going to be burnt with the rest, and I had it made into a table: the only thing left of the old Nausicaa, along with my memories.

I was able to salvage the trunk of a Jacaranda tree.